Personal Power

Personal Power

Gillian Stokes

MQP
MQ Publications Ltd

Published by MQ Publications Limited
12 The Ivories, 6–8 Northampton Street, London N1 2HY
Tel: 020 7359 2244 / Fax: 020 7359 1616
email: mail@mqpublications.com

Copyright © MQ Publications Limited 2002

Text © Gillian Stokes 2002
Design: Philippa Jarvis

ISBN: 1-84072-423-4

3 5 7 9 0 8 6 4 2

Printed and bound in China

Permissions have been sought where possible for all quotations used.
Please contact the company for any information regarding these.

Contents

	Preface	6
Chapter One	*Know Thyself*	11
	Discover What You Want from Life	14
	What's Holding You Back?	18
	Choosing Power	24
	Your Approach to Life	34
Chapter Two	*Your Environment*	39
	The Media	44
	Personal Preconceptions	48
	Who Are You?	56
	False Assumptions	64
Chapter Three	*Beginnings*	71
	Access Intuition	74
	Maintain Calm	80
	Commitment	86
Chapter Four	*Work in Progress*	91
	Positive Speech	92
	Walk Tall	96
	Speak with Confidence	100
	Examine Your Attitudes	106
	Willpower	112
Chapter Five	*Evaluation*	115
	Coping with Disappointment	120
	Success and How to Cope with It	122
	Accept Praise	126
	Credits	128

Preface

**❝ Knowledge comes, but wisdom lingers. ❞**

ALFRED LORD TENNYSON

*P*ersonal power stems from healthy self-esteem. When we feel good about ourselves and embrace our talents and resources, we have taken the first steps toward realizing our full potential. Perhaps you shy away from the thought of power because you see it as a negative force, to be used against others. Consider looking at power a little differently. When we express personal power positively, we acknowledge and value our network of loving and responsible relationships.

We may have many reasons for not claiming the power that is our birthright. In some cases, others may have discouraged us from developing self-esteem, independence, and initiative in our earliest years. Consequently, self-denial became a habit. Some adults are unable to encourage or support the emotional development of the children in their care, in part because they experienced little support during their own childhood. Unchecked, this lack can play out generation after generation. A caregiver who has lacked early emotional support, for whatever reason, may interpret a child's gradual expression of independence as threatening to his or her fragile sense of power and authority. Some adults see any sign of a child's independence as threatening; they fear the child may no longer love and depend on them. Unable to view a child's movement toward independence as a positive and healthy expression of individualism, they try to hinder or suppress acts of creativity and confidence. In doing so, they squash the natural development of personal power.

Others negatively equate personal power with the assertion of power over others, a trait few would like to associate with themselves. We

distrust our power because we don't want others to see us as overbearing. Or we may fear public exposure of any kind because it can lead to the risk of criticism. Perhaps we lacked encouragement or the means to seize opportunities in childhood.

Wise mentors and leaders embody the virtue of non-competition. It is not that they don't love to compete, but they do so in the spirit of play. In this they are like children and in harmony with the Tao. They encourage all within their sphere of influence to develop their strengths.

When you discover and tap into your personal power, you can develop your full potential. The benefits touch all those who interact with you. Whatever your past, you possess a powerful inner spirit worthy of exploration. You can approach the future with a different sense of yourself. Your personal power will contribute to your growth, to the health of your relationships, and to your wider society. You require a high degree of awareness and flexibility to balance your own and others' needs and wishes. Live your life authentically, in harmony with others, and you will live for everyone's benefit. The acts of many individuals create society. You can choose to become an inspiration to others while fulfilling your dreams.

If a man is respectful he will not be treated with insolence. If he is tolerant he will win the multitude. If he is trustworthy in word his fellow men will entrust him with responsibility. If he is quick he will achieve results. If he is generous he will be good enough to be put in a position over his fellow men.

CONFUCIUS

Know
Thyself

“*A man who knows he is a fool is not a great fool.*”

CHUANG-TSE

*I*n order to release your personal power, you need to become better acquainted with yourself—better acquainted and better friends. The key to accessing power is self-knowledge. Think about your life for a moment. In an ideal world, where would you choose to be in ten years time? In twenty years? Thirty? Now contemplate what your life would look like if no "what ifs?" and "buts" stood in your way. What makes you laugh? What claims your passionate

attention? What activities cause you to lose all sense of time? Unless you know the answers to some of these questions, you face the danger of drifting through life, driven by the wind that blows the strongest. Don't allow yourself to become one who, nearing death, regrets what you might have done if only you had taken a few risks. We each have a purpose in life. It may seem a quiet note in the overall symphony of life, but without it the music would lack its richness.

> 66 *Never lose your self-respect, nor be too familiar with yourself when you are alone. Let your integrity itself be your own standard of rectitude, and be more indebted to the severity of your own judgment of yourself than to all external precepts. Desist from unseemly conduct, rather out of respect for your own virtue than for the strictures of external authority.* 99

BALTASAR GRACIÁN

43

Discover What You Want from Life

66 The world is all gates, all opportunities, strings of tension waiting to be struck. 99

RALPH WALDO EMERSON

*a*ccessing your personal power starts with having a clear idea of what you want from life. Focus on what you want, not what you think others want for you. It may take a bit of work to differentiate the two. The following steps will get you started.

- Face the facts. What must change in order to achieve your goals?

- Make plans. What small steps would move you toward your long-term goals? What options do you have?

- Daydream. Imagine that you have achieved your goals. Allow this fantasy to return whenever you have a quiet moment: waiting for an appointment, commuting on the bus or train. Just shut your eyes and live your dream. The more often you visit any idea, the more focused you will become, enabling you to recognize and seize opportunities.

- Prepare for external limitations. What might prevent you from achieving your goals and where do these things spring from? Consider how you can overcome them.

- Examine internal barriers. Are you too scared to take risks? Resolve to make your own decisions. You will have to extend your comfort zone in order to make progress.

- Think positively. Tap into the power of positive thought and language to reinforce your desires. Eliminate *trying* and substitute *doing*.

- Trust your intuition.

- Do not compromise. Maintain your ideals and standards; success gained at the cost of integrity is no success at all.

- Know that you already possess personal power. No outside source can bestow power on you or deprive you of it.

Why do you want personal power? Do you crave success, wealth, relationships, fame? Perhaps you dream of finding the cure for cancer or becoming a great philanthropist or benefactor. Unless you clarify what you want from your life, you will never attain it. Your success is only limited by your goals. Once you become clear about what you want from life, you can focus on how to achieve your aims. The longest journey really does start with just one step.

When you know the extent of your ambition, you can set about defining how to achieve it. Ignore any negative thoughts; that you are too clumsy, too stupid, too old, too poor, too late, too whatever to accomplish your goals. The universe can't wait to dance with you; you just need to call the tune. Until you do, it cannot respond with what you want. Become clear in your own mind and you will become clear in word and deed. Your energies will become focused, and the universe will respond to your call.

The next time that you have a spontaneous urge to do something, indulge it, providing that it won't endanger anyone's well-being. Imagine yourself enacting that fleeting dream. Where would it take

66 Things are neither good nor bad but thinking makes them so. 99

WILLIAM SHAKESPEARE

you? Envision yourself in a role or situation that would fulfill your dream. Imagine yourself as successful and in control. Be specific. Don't merely decide upon some generality, such as, "I want to be rich," or "I want to be in love." Imagine how you could become wealthy or how you could bring love into your life.

What secret dream have you protected from exposure or ridicule? What have you always suspected you might have done, if only…? Pursue these buried longings and aspirations. Once you uncover and embrace them, you will be amazed how things will unfold for you. See this as play, not as work. You already know your power, deep down. Now you have a chance to set it free.

What's Holding You Back?

“ We must not weep for what we might have been. There is still time. ”

EDWARD MATCHETT

Too often we choose to focus on the disadvantages we believe have kept us from reaching our goals. We shift our focus from what we claim to want from life to the relative safety of the familiar: the litany of reasons why our dreams are impossible. At such times we do not own personal power; we fall back on those excuses that save us from effort, exposure, fear of ridicule, or the failure that may follow a decision to act. Though we may see ourselves as victims of our circumstances, we could become victors, people who succeed when presented with challenges. We must simply make a choice.

Until you learn to recognize your habitual excuses, you will likely continue to avoid the challenges that might take you nearer to your goals. But as you gain insight, you will come to realize that you have other choices, if you wish to make them. This does not mean you will act differently every time you have a choice. Over time, as you treat yourself with compassion and strengthen your determination to succeed, you will find it easier to take risks.

Do not criticize yourself or despair when you feel unable to take a forward step. There is no reason to become your own stern critic. You probably already have enough disapproving voices in your life. Be compassionate. Learn to recognize your reluctance as an understandable avoidance of pain or fear of exposure. Greet these reactions as old friends, smile to yourself, and decide whether today things might change. The choice is yours.

❝ *A monkey was carrying two handfuls of peas. One little pea dropped out. He tried to pick it up, and spilt twenty. He tried to pick up the twenty, and spilt them all. Then he lost his temper, scattered the peas in all directions, and ran away.* **❞**

LEO TOLSTOY

We all use aggression, manipulation, and anger on occasion, yet almost always in doing so, we lose personal power. You know whether you have a tendency to respond with an unreasonably quick temper or aggressiveness. You may even have learned to see it as an asset, as a way to defend yourself. However, if you can learn new habits—to become assertive rather than aggressive or angry—you will gain others' respect and achieve far more. Those who resort to aggression and bullying to achieve their goals reveal their lack of real power. Little dogs tend to yap incessantly; the big ones know their power. While bullies may often win in the short term, the resentment and lack of respect they inspire will eventually undermine them. The following tale illustrates the point:

A woman once took a job cleaning a private home to earn extra cash. The homeowner constantly bullied and spied on her, presumably because she didn't trust the cleaner around her valuables. Her children also treated the housecleaner with distrust. Most hurtful, she forbade the housecleaner to use any of the many toilets in the house (did the homeowner fear contamination?). Retaliation became inevitable. The housecleaner took her revenge one day as she cleaned a bathroom, unsupervised. She discovered her employer's face cloth, used it to clean the toilet, and replaced it for the homeowner's continued use.

Not commendable assertive behavior, but perhaps quite satisfying. However, if the employee had taken more control over her personal power, this scene need not have occurred.

When sensing her employer's mistrust, the housecleaner might have politely questioned the homeowner's close observation of her work, placing the onus on her employer in order to justify herself. Had the

conversation gone further, the woman might have reminded her employer of her excellent references and encouraged the employer to check them, thereby reclaiming control. If such questioning lead the homeowner to fire the woman for her impertinence, would she have suffered a large loss? On the other hand, if the housecleaner really needed the job, she could have chosen to tolerate her employer's eccentricities, knowing that she was permitting them to continue. In making such a conscious decision, she would have removed the level of annoyance that led to her unsanitary retaliation.

> **66** *What lies in our power to do,*
> *it lies in our power not to do.* **99**
>
> ARISTOTLE

Choosing Power

❝ The more prohibitions you have,
the less virtuous people will be. ❞

ANONYMOUS

The fear of losing control creates stress. The late Italian psychoanalyst, Roberto Assagioli, the founder of the psychological method Psychosynthesis, Psychology with a Soul, described an example of maintaining control despite adversity. In 1938 he was imprisoned by the fascists in Italy for his unpopular political beliefs. Deprived of his liberty, Assagioli described how he discovered freedom in acceptance, despite living in what appeared to be a powerless state.

I realized I was free to take one of many attitudes toward the situation, to give one value or another to it, to utilize it in one way or another. I could rebel inwardly and curse; or I could submit passively, vegetating; or I could indulge in the unwholesome pleasure of self-pity and assume the martyr's role; or I could take the situation in a sporting way and with a sense of humor, considering it as a novel and interesting experience. ...I could make of it a rest cure or a period of intense thinking, either about personal matters — reviewing my past life and pondering on it — or about scientific and philosophical problems; or I could take advantage of the situation to undertake personal psychological training; or, finally, I could make it into a spiritual retreat. I had the clear, pure perception that this was entirely my own affair; that I was free to choose any or several of these attitudes.

ROBERTO ASSAGIOLI, *FREEDOM IN JAIL*

Freedom of choice can also work counterproductively. You can actually limit your possibilities by choosing to dwell on fearful thoughts, on what you lack, on what you believe you cannot do, on a difficult environment, or on memories of past hurts. Or you can choose to rise above them. Choose carefully and wisely.

66 *Experience is not what happens to you, it is what you do with what happens to you.* **99**

ALDOUS HUXLEY

Manipulation is just another form of aggression; in attempting to manipulate another, you deny that person respect. Such actions reveal to any wise observer that you lack personal power. While manipulation may lead to immediate gains, it will likely bring long-term losses. Anyone who has borne the brunt of your actions will have difficulty trusting you in the future. If instead you have a strong sense of your own worth and of that of those around you, you will choose not to resort to this unrewarding strategy.

In recognizing your responsibilities to others and acting from awareness and compassion, you can truly exhibit personal power. Powerfully assertive transactions include those that express honest

feelings, acknowledge the feelings and needs of others, and clearly state intentions. If you must deny the wishes of another, act from personal power and do so with no false excuses, no insincere promises that merely make the task less distasteful. Conversely, if you find yourself in the position of accepting an offer, do so with grace and appreciation. Make a genuine commitment to complete the tasks you undertake. Say yes when you mean yes and no when you mean no and have the courage to realize your right to state either in any situation.

In a speech Abraham Lincoln delivered at the height of the Civil War, he referred to the Southerners as fellow human beings who were in error. An elderly lady chastised him for not calling them irreconcilable enemies who must be destroyed. "Why, madam," Lincoln replied, "do I not destroy my enemies when I make them my friends?"

ROBERT GREENE

> **❝ If you want to govern the people, you must place yourself below them. If you want to lead the people, you must learn how to follow them. ❞**
>
> LAO-TZU

If you must bear bad news, you may have no-control over the content of your message. But you can, and should, exercise control over how you impart that information. Candid but compassionate honesty can soften the blow. Be tactful about when and where you choose to speak, if possible. Be direct, free from personal bias, and willing to offer support or to give the recipient some time alone, if necessary. Often an offer of practical assistance can help, such as offering to drive someone home, to collect children from school, to supply a hot meal, or whatever seems appropriate in the situation.

If you must criticize someone, be constructive and to the point. Restrict yourself to criticism of specific behavior. Own the statements you make, prefacing your statements with "I..." rather than making them impersonal and abstract. Ask for feedback and listen carefully. Perhaps a simple explanation will change your position. Be firm but considerate in your dealings with others and most will cooperate with you—be nasty, and know that most will seek revenge. You choose; would you prefer allies or enemies?

❝ *Those who know don't talk.* *Those who talk don't know.* ❞

ANONYMOUS

How do you react when someone criticizes you? Can you allow yourself to learn from constructive criticism? If you believe the criticism is genuinely misplaced or relies on factual errors, politely point these out. Do not enter into a tit-for-tat argument. If you have a point, make it simply and, if possible, suggest how to fix the problem.

66 *Let us be brave in the face of adversity.* 99

MARCUS ANNAEUS SENECA

If someone directs criticism against you on a personal level rather than on a constructive one, try to diffuse the situation. Gently point out that you would like to come to a solution, and then direct the conversation to the issue at hand.

66 *'How can one inculcate in the common people the virtue of reverence, of doing their best and of enthusiasm?'*

The Master said, 'Rule over them with dignity and they will be reverent; treat them with kindness and they will do their best; raise the good and instruct those who are backward and they will be imbued with enthusiasm.' 99

CONFUCIUS

If you know that a critical confrontation is imminent, it is important that you prepare yourself. Consider the issue and what might be said, from the least criticism to the worst possible attack, and rehearse your responses. You will then retain your confidence and security when the confrontation occurs. Even if the worst possible scenario plays out, you will know what you wish to say and do. By exercising control and being aware of your choices, your personal power remains undiminished.

We cannot learn assertive behavior overnight. Practice making the effort to monitor your dealings with people and to act with clarity and dignity. As often as you can, treat others as you would like them to treat you. You will reap the rewards.

> **“ *Self-confidence is the first requisite to great undertakings.* ”**
>
> SAMUEL JOHNSON

Your Approach to Life

❝ *There is just one life for each of us: our own.* ❞

EURIPIDES

To make the most of your personal power, it helps to understand your working nature. Think about how you approach life. Are you able to recognize yourself in any of the following light-hearted descriptions? While you might resonate with some aspects from each type, which one do you identify with the most?

Calm and Organized: You have extremely tidy sock and underwear drawers and you remember every family birthday. You know your bank account balance without even having to check. You rarely run out of essential supplies, and your car has never run out of gas. When you travel, you plan your route meticulously and set off with plenty of time.

Free-floating: You allow yourself to be inspired by whatever chance brings your way. You love the challenge of learning new things and are so adaptable that you change your plans at a moment's notice. You tend to leave a job just before receiving a promotion to a more responsible role. You are easily bored.

Crisis-driven: You work best on a deadline and always leave things to the last minute. You often lose things because your desk is a riot of files and papers. You prefer to party late, sleep in, and pay the price in rushing to get to work on time. When life gets a little dull, you spice it up with a drama or two: a move, a new job, a confrontation, or a spending spree. You have rashly walked out of relationships and lived to regret your actions.

Each of these personality types has charm, but unconscious habits can drain our potential for personal power. Consider whether your

behavior is working for, or against, the fulfillment of your dreams. You may have learned your style from others without ever questioning it. Try the following: For one week, act with conscious awareness. Pay attention to your interactions with the world. You may decide to make some permanent changes to your behavior, or you may choose to keep your present style.

66 Of all the paths a man could strike into, there is, at any given moment, a best path... a thing which, here and now, it were of all things wisest for him to do... to find this path, and walk in it, is the one thing needful for him. 99

THOMAS CARLYLE

The Crown. Place it upon your head and you assume a different pose—tranquil yet radiating assurance. Never show doubt, never lose your dignity beneath the crown, or it will not fit. It will seem to be destined for one more worthy. Do not wait for a coronation; the greatest emperors crown themselves.

ROBERT GREENE

Your
Environment

> ❝ *A wise man will make more opportunities than he finds.* ❞
>
> FRANCIS BACON

*P*ersonal power reflects a tremendous inner confidence and awareness, but the outer environment also profoundly affects our inner states. This reciprocal relationship also affects our expression of power. In mystical texts, "As above, so below" refers to this relationship between the tangible and the intangible.

You do not need any particular physical or social attributes to realize your personal power. It does not come about as a matter of luck or intelligence, the right family connections, or a good education. Such apparent advantages may actually prevent people from realizing their personal power. They may harbor the suspicion that their success depends on things beyond their control. When wealth commands obedience, poverty becomes fearsome. When good looks guarantee attention, healthy ageing can seem threatening. Any advantage that depends on an outer source or circumstance, such as the praise and envy of others, can disappear in an instant. True personal power arises from an inner strength, whatever the outer circumstance.

66 *If powerful men and women could remain centered in the Tao, all things would be in harmony. The world would become a paradise. All people would be at peace, and the law would be written in their hearts.* 99

LAO-TZU

44

❝ If one advances confidently in the direction of his dreams, and endeavors to live the life which he has imagined, he will meet with a success unexpected in common hours. ❞

HENRY DAVID THOREAU

Your personal power can be of benefit to others as well as to yourself. You may choose to express yourself through community action on a local, national, or even global scale. Whatever the extent of your interaction, have the courage to be honest about your needs and capabilities. We are all flawed—even the most confident among us—so you do not have to hide any part of yourself. All you must be is what you are, yourself. That is enough, in spite of what other people may wish you to believe. Neither must your stage be impressive or your audience large. Perhaps you will say the right thing in a chance remark to someone at a bus stop. You may never know that you have done so, but your words might change a life forever.

Set high standards for yourself and adhere to them, whatever the nature of your work. You will become aware that small things do make a difference. You will gain in personal satisfaction, feel less stressed, and become more effective and helpful to others.

66 *Every day I examine myself on three counts. In what I have undertaken on another's behalf, have I failed to do my best? In my dealings with my friends have I failed to be trustworthy in what I say? Have I passed on to others anything that I have not tried out myself?* 99

TSENG TZU

The Media

❝Space we can recover, time never.❞

NAPOLEON BONAPARTE

All forms of media can function as useful resource tools, but all too often we lack the self-discipline to use them effectively. Without self-awareness we may fritter away our potential. Passive observation then replaces our will and actions. We become more absorbed in the dramas of others' lives than in our own. If you want personal power, then get busy making the news, not watching or reading about it.

Our daily dose of news and entertainment, gleaned from the television, newspapers, multimedia, and the Internet, can become a huge waste of time. We will never discover personal power through third-hand observation. It requires life and personal input. Television in particular represents an insidious chewing gum for the mind; those who intend to realize their personal power should limit the time they spend absorbing media output. The great psychoanalyst Carl Gustav Jung expressed his dismay at the prospect of a society that has constant access to television. He recognized how seductive and hypnotic the medium might become.

Try this experiment. Turn off the television and radio and stop reading newspapers and magazines for a week. Do it for a month if you are made of sterner stuff. Notice how much more time you suddenly have free to pursue those activities that you've put off until "later." You may well experience boredom and disorientation at first, especially during the hours of your favorite television shows or when you would normally settle down to read the newspaper or do the crossword. Persevere. Divert yourself from these anxieties by making good use of

your new-found time. Take some of the first steps toward identifying and realizing your life goals. Get in touch with your personal power. After your experimental media "fast," you may discover you can use the media in a positive manner, rather than be used by or subjected to it. Fine, reintroduce it in small doses, but remember your life is your greatest gift. Don't fritter it away passively.

66 *Nothing can bring you peace but yourself.* 99

RALPH WALDO EMERSON

Personal Preconceptions

66 *What the caterpillar calls the end of the world the master calls the butterfly.* 99

ANONYMOUS

Our expectations can determine what we are able to achieve. While you cannot make the world flat by simply believing that it is so, such a belief would certainly limit your travel plans. In a similar way, what we expect of other people may color our perceptions of them. If we stereotype, judge, or scapegoat someone, perhaps based on nothing more concrete than superficial appearance, we prejudice our interactions with them from the start. In the same way, we may limit ourselves in what we assume we can and cannot do. As we think, so we become, and as we learn, so we think. Stretch a bit. Don't become limited by your own perception or imagination. Our expectations shape our experience and the world we inhabit.

66 Vex not thy spirit at the course of things; they heed not thy vexation. How ludicrous and outlandish is astonishment at anything that may happen in life. 99

MARCUS AURELIUS

So, why do we not aspire to more? All too often we continue, long into adulthood, to obey the dictates and mimic the beliefs of our childhood caregivers and teachers. Our present-day doctors, lawyers, and politicians, and close family members also represent powerful

> ❝ *To achieve what you have never achieved, do what you have never done.* ❞
>

sources of peer pressure. Do you live your life limited by others' expectations? In doing so, you give away your personal power. When we rely too heavily on others instead of making our own choices, we act from fear and experience weakness.

Do any of these voices sound familiar?

"You will never amount to anything."

"Look at you, who is going to want to marry you?"

"One day you will take over the family firm."

"All rich folks are mean. That's how they get to be rich."

"No one in our family can sing."

"Our family has produced doctors for six generations."

"One day you will marry a nice Jewish girl and make your mother happy."

"No one will ever take care of you as well as your mother."

"You call yourself a dancer? You have two left feet."

In all likelihood, you can supply your own list. But where do such statements leave the doctor's daughter who dreams of becoming an engineer or the boy who longs to sing professionally? For that matter, how could a philanthropist fund worthwhile projects if he or she didn't make the money in the first place? The mentors who shaped our expectations probably meant well and doubtless did not realize the lasting effect of their words. Did you ever question what made them so sure of who you might become? You owe it to yourself and to the world to experience your true potential and exercise your greatest gift—your free will. Why not claim your personal power and work toward achieving goals determined solely by you?

66 True happiness, we are told, consists in getting out of one's self, but the point is not only to get out; you must stay out, and to stay out, you must have some absorbing errand. 99

HENRY JAMES

If a child lives with criticism,
    He learns to condemn,
If a child lives with hostility,
    He learns to fight,
If a child lives with ridicule,
    He learns to be shy,
If a child lives with shame,
    He learns to feel guilty,
If a child lives with tolerance,
    He learns to be patient,
If a child lives with
encouragement,
    He learns confidence,

If a child lives with praise,
    He learns to appreciate,
If a child lives with fairness,
    He learns justice,
If a child lives with security,
    He learns to have faith,
If a child lives with approval,
    He learns to like himself,
If a child lives with
acceptance and friendship,
    He learns to find love in
the world.

DOROTHY LAW HOLTE

53

❝Learn
what you are
and be such.**❞**

PINDAR

Who Are You?

❝As you go through life make this your goal, keep your eye upon the doughnut and not upon the hole.❞

DOUGHNUT CAFÉ, MELBOURNE

*I*f you feel the time has come to make your own choices, how will you go about it? Well, you could do worse than to start by nurturing yourself. Get to know what you like and dislike. Pamper yourself; you don't need to spend a lot of money. Treat yourself to a hot bath by candlelight or a quiet hour in the park. If you live a harried, overachieving life, such simple luxuries might amaze you. If you tend toward the quiet and obedient type, perhaps you should try a taste of responsible recklessness. If you rarely feel heard, write a letter to the press, or contact a radio phone-in show regarding a subject that inflames your passion. Perhaps you need to renegotiate your current situation with someone. Believe in the validity of your opinion. If expressing yourself seems daunting, consider taking a class in assertiveness. Whatever your inspiration, make your voice public as the adult you are, without apology or favor. You may feel shy and nervous at the prospect but you will become exhilarated and empowered when you discover that others value your opinion. You can negotiate changes in your life.

Take stock of your present situation. Do others depend on you? If so, tell them about any changes you want to make. Involve your friends and family, especially if your plans will affect them. You may discover a willing support team when you include others. Family and friends will less likely feel threatened if you confide in, consult, and include them. Explain why you feel the need to make changes in your life and how a happier you will benefit them. Remember, however, to use discretion. For example, if you would like to explore other career opportunities and

> ❝ *The life which is unexamined is not worth living.* ❞
>
> PLATO

you share your dreams with your present employer too soon, you may find yourself on the job market a little sooner!

Can you live in a clutter-free, minimalist environment, or do you need the stimulation of lots of stuff? The Eastern art of Feng Shui demonstrates how the location and nature of objects and our interactions with them affects us, positively and negatively. Perhaps you live surrounded by things that convey emotional memories. If they cause you pain, consider getting rid of your emotional clutter. If old letters or photographs upset you when you rediscover them in the back of that drawer, why keep them? Do not feel obliged to torture yourself. If you do not already hold your loved ones in your heart and mind, what purpose do the objects you associate with them serve? Once you free yourself from the evidence of the past, you can get to know and reinvent yourself. You may find it painful to part with certain reminders, but if you feel sure of no regrets, make a bonfire of this worthless, yet emotionally charged memorabilia and see how incredibly liberating it feels. Consciously bid each item farewell, honoring the experience its memory brought you, whether for good or ill, then throw it into the bonfire or the trash.

66 We should know what our convictions are, and stand for them. Upon one's own philosophy, conscious or unconscious, depends one's ultimate interpretation of facts. Therefore it is wise to be as clear as possible about one's subjective principles. As the man is, so will be his ultimate truth. 99

CARL JUNG

66 *Sometimes it is more important to discover what one cannot do, than what one can.* **99**

LIN YUTANG

However, if you harbor any doubt that you can make an irrevocable separation—or you want certain items for future generations—remove such emotionally loaded things by storing them securely out of sight in an attic, basement, or garage. Or give valuables that hold painful associations to someone for whom they have no negative connotations to look after or enjoy. Get them out of your sight, so you can start again, free of any backward trails.

If you do decide to keep such things, perhaps to give to your children when they have grown, you can still make a ceremonial separation from your past. Substitute pinecones, acorns, or other small tokens for the events or people you associate with the things you have stored away.

Treat each token in turn to the ceremonial bonfire or garbage can, first investing it with the past experience or the emotional tie. For example, suppose your mother died before you resolved a difficult childhood, which left you with a mixture of anger and regret. As you hold the token that represents your past with her, you might let it go by saying, "Thank you for bringing me into this world, Mother. I'm sorry we didn't get along better when we were together but now I must make my own way. I release you from the emotional ties that bound us and forgive you for the difficult times we shared, as I hope you forgive me." Now toss the token and the past it represents into the flames or the garbage. You will not hurt your late mother with this ceremony. However, if you sincerely imbue the act with meaning, you will lighten your emotional burden.

To know oneself, one should assert oneself.

ALBERT CAMUS

❝There is a vitality, a life force that is translated through you into action. And because there is only one of you in all time, this expression is unique, and if you block it, it will never exist through any other medium and be lost.❞

MARTHA GRAHAM

False Assumptions

❝ Nature arms each man with some faculty which enables him to do easily some feat impossible to any other. ❞

RALPH WALDO EMERSON

We make many false assumptions merely because we have never really befriended ourselves. Have you ever tried to question your choice of favorite color or flower? Perhaps you have always said you like blue best merely because your father said it was his favorite. Did you ever question whether you really prefer blue? Have you surrounded yourself with things that reflect another's preferences, a partner's or parent's for example, rather than your own? Would a different color scheme make you happier? Become aware of the colors that please you and experiment. You can clarify your preferences by doodling with paints or crayons. Do not worry about your artistic ability, just play. No one will see your drawings. Pay attention to which crayons you use the most. Does your preference vary based on your day, your mood, your obligations? See if you can associate particular colors with certain emotions. Does black reflect a negative day for you? Or does it have an entirely different meaning for you? Perhaps you find it calming or even uplifting. Become aware of your associations. Don't lock yourself into associating colors with someone else's expected meanings. When you know how colors affect you, you can begin to select and use them to encourage and promote specific qualities in your life.

Do you dream in color? If you dream of a particular hue, you may find it interesting to research the symbolic meaning generally attached to that color. Compare your interpretation of your dream to the conventional interpretation. Do you see a message in either? Notice the colors around you: those worn by others, plastered on a billboard, hung in an art gallery, or evident in nature. Which draw your attention the

most? How do you feel when you introduce these colors into your home or office? Perhaps it would help to wear or otherwise consciously bring the color of your dreams into your life for a while. When you wear the colors that attract you, you may find your mood lifted. If it brings you warmth and happiness, extend your interaction with your chosen color in whatever way you feel inspired.

Can you refurnish or redecorate your home or, less expensively, purchase art in your colors and display it where you live or work? If you long to change your environment totally, hang pictures of the countryside, the city, or the sea where you will see them frequently. Replace the pictures periodically so you don't come to take them for granted. Before you rush to redecorate your apartment with cerise paint, try a vase of flowers as a less drastic way to experiment with color. Or perhaps you could try new drapes, a new carpet, or a new hat. Begin to use color to create a mood. Maybe a red suit, silk scarf, or necktie will emphasize the attitude you need for an upcoming meeting or appointment. If you are naturally exuberant, a gray suit or tie might help to reinforce an air of dignity. Use clothing to reflect and reinforce your intentions. If new clothes are beyond your means, smaller objects can serve to inspire you with their energy. For example, try investing a small

*66**If you want to succeed,
double your failure rate.**99*

TOM WATSON, JR., CHAIRMAN **IBM**

stone or other token with the qualities you would like to strengthen in yourself—perhaps the ability to speak your mind clearly. Then, before a difficult meeting, you might boost your confidence by slipping that small stone into your pocket. You can touch this token for reassurance whenever you need it during the meeting. It may sound like a silly thing, but to a nervous person, such small acts can help. After a series of more successful encounters, you will find you do not need such props.

These are simple changes you can make to boost your personal power. As you become more confident in any situation, you will exude that confidence and gain respect. As you enjoy more respect, you will feel more emboldened to act. The smallest acts of taking control, of exercising choice, can turn your life around.

67

> **❝ Nothing would be done at all if a man waited until he could do it so well that no one could find fault with it. ❞**
>
> CARDINAL NEWMAN

Have you ever noticed that those who seem the most positive in their outlook, the "can-do" types, also tend to achieve the most? These people know their personal power, and they know how to use it. They may have difficulties as well, of course, but they are not limited by them. They don't define themselves by what they cannot do, or waste a lot of energy in trying to convince others that they can do everything. Rather, they know how to make a problem into an opportunity for growth and how to anticipate a positive outcome despite difficulties. They do not allow things others might regard as problems—phobias, physical disabilities, a less than ideal childhood or education—to limit them. The more we do, the more we can do, it seems. You will not have the deadening inertia of stagnation to overcome if you keep yourself active.

If you experience yourself as a truly free person there is nothing you cannot achieve. Most of the limitations that we experience in our lives are a product of what we believe and intend, and of how we experience ourselves. Consider for a moment: Other than automatic functions, such as breathing, what have you ever done that you did not first consciously decide to do? The smallest infants quickly learn that a smile or cry will get them what they need. Later, their willpower will fuel their urge to crawl and walk. You would be unable to stand and walk across a room if you did not know how to exercise your will.

Nothing in the world is more flexible and yielding than water. Yet when it attacks the firm and the strong, none can withstand it, because they have no way to change it. So the flexible overcome the adamant, the yielding overcome the forceful. Everyone knows this, but no one can do it.

LAO-TZU

Beginnings

"And the trouble is, if you don't risk anything, you risk even more."

ERICA JONG

Set yourself realistic targets, regarding each as a step toward a greater goal. Perhaps you need to take some classes to become qualified for a certain profession. As the saying goes: God may supply the acorns, but He will not throw them into a squirrel's nest. You must make the effort, but when you work toward your own goals, effort need not feel like work. You may find joy in it. Be prepared to face moments of self-doubt and the setbacks that attend every journey. What may seem like setbacks may just be the spurs and motivators that test your will and bring you the lessons you need to learn.

When our own efforts bring us what we want, self-esteem and confidence grows, and with it our ability to become more assertive and successful in the future. On the other hand, a lack of self-esteem breeds loss of confidence. We may then act out of fear, aggression, defensiveness, or apology, each with less chance of success. Failure feeds into a downward spiral of lowered self-esteem, lowered confidence, and less success. You choose. Do you want fear and failure to motivate you, or would you rather take some degree of risk to discover how successful you can be?

"Come to the edge!"
"No we cannot, we are afraid."
"Come to the edge!"
"No we cannot, we'll fall."
"Come to the edge!"
And they came, and he pushed them, and they flew!

APOLLINAIRE

Access Intuition

❝ When you let intuition have its way with you, you open up new levels of the world. Such opening-up is the most practical of all activities. ❞

EVELYN UNDERHILL

Everyone has some degree of intuition that can be encouraged and developed. Perhaps you've had the experience of straining in vain to remember someone's name or phone number, only to have the fact pop into your mind once you've turned your attention elsewhere. Or maybe, while reading a book, driving the car, or washing dishes, you've suddenly realized the answer to a problem you had put out of your mind. If an answer doesn't come immediately, sometimes it's beneficial to let the mind go off on its own tangents. You can learn to use your intuition to discover what you truly want from life.

The intuitive experience is characterized by an honesty and clarity, and we can learn to distinguish it from directed, wishful thinking. Some people refer to intuition as the language of the heart; it often suggests a different kind of response than our reasoning, socially shaped self might present. An intuitive response, the fleeting alignment of your personal truth, differs from purposeful, manufactured thought. When you consciously work on an idea, developing your thoughts, you are not using your intuition. You can recognize intuition by its simplicity, immediacy, and aptness. You may feel a "rightness" and unexpectedness in an intuitive response. It seems to well up from an unfettered and truthful part of yourself; it comes from beyond the learned *oughts* and *shoulds* that normally dictate reasoned response. Intuitive reactions may seem mischievous at times, and at others, mystical or even religious. Whatever its style, within the intuitive response you will discover a clue to the direction that your truest self would choose, if it were allowed free reign.

If you find it difficult to recognize your intuitive voice, try the following exercise. Even practicing for ten minutes a day may bring you benefit. Pick a time and a place when you can be quiet, undisturbed, and fully aware. (Perhaps this is a lofty goal in itself!) Allow yourself to feel relaxed and still, breathing evenly, then ask yourself silently or aloud what you need to know. Do not attempt to reason out a suitable answer. If your mind wanders into irrelevant thoughts and daydreams, gently return to the question and wait patiently for a reply. After a while, move on with your day.

Contemplate only one subject per session. Don't get into a jumble of ideas. Allow yourself plenty of time for a response before getting back to your day. You may not discover an answer until after your session,

66A man should not strive to eliminate his complexes but to get into accord with them, for they are legitimately what directs his conduct in the world.99

SIGMUND FREUD

A crow, ready to die with thirst, flew with joy to a Pitcher, which he saw at a distance. But when he came up to it, he found the water so low that with all his stooping and straining he was unable to reach it. Thereupon he tried to break the Pitcher; then to overturn it; but his strength was not sufficient to do either. At last, seeing some small pebbles lying near the place, he cast them one by one into the Pitcher and thus by degrees, raised the water up to the very brim, and quenched his thirst.

AESOP

perhaps even several days later. If no answer comes to mind, don't worry. You have "lit a beacon" that will attract a response. When you act in tune with your intuition, you greatly magnify your chance of success. Focus on aligning with your innate nature, at a level where you have no doubts about who you are or about your personal power. Remember that the first thought that pops into your head, no matter how irrelevant it may seem, is important. Some say that the first thought we have comes from God.

" *For him who has no concentration, there is no tranquility.* "

THE BHAGAVAD GITA

Maintain Calm

" Great events make me quiet and calm;
it is only trifles that irritate my nerves. "

QUEEN VICTORIA

Domination, particularly when it is used in business interactions, can abuse personal power. Certain managers, when dealing with a subordinate or job candidate, will place the underling at a disadvantage in order to emphasize their control. Such managers may force others to wait as a subtle signal of their dominance. They may play other games as well; when they grant an audience, they may make a subordinate understand his or her lack of importance through something as simple as the arrangement of furniture. You can rise above such well-known and somewhat bullying tactics by drawing on your personal power. You don't need to act in kind, and no one may even notice your actions, but neither do you need to feel intimidated. Here are some tips, for judicious use, to exercise your personal power.

Spend your time in the waiting room thinking through a problem or planning the rest of your day. Focus on something that will keep you from watching the clock. Make notes. Open your briefcase, and spend more energy on your papers than on the fact you have been kept waiting. When called, replace your papers and gather your thoughts. Do not become flustered, embarrassed, or apologetic if your interviewer must wait a moment for you, but do not dawdle.

❝ *He who is of calm and happy nature will hardly feel the pressure of age, but to him who is of an opposite disposition, youth and age are equally a burden.* ❞

PLATO

Once you have entered the meeting room, if you are offered a seat in a disadvantageous position, move it to a better location providing this doesn't cause too much disruption. Alternatively, say that you prefer to stand. However, do not become pushy. If you don't see a quick and immediate fix, recognize the power play for what it is and refuse to become intimidated.

If your hands feel shaky, decline any offer of coffee or water. Also decline a cigarette or cigar. Such an offer may be intended to reveal whether you have addictive habits rather than being offered as an act of generosity. Do not fidget or show nervousness, even if you feel it. Remember to breathe deeply and evenly. Keep in mind that you have entered an artificial situation, and counter each move in a calmly controlled manner, without aggression. Ask some questions yourself. Know that you have a right to this audience and that you have a voice worth hearing. Resolve to act from the awareness you have gained about yourself. When you take responsibility for your thoughts, beliefs, and actions, you claim your personal power. Aim to be assertive but not manipulative in your interactions with others. When you have the confidence to act assertively rather than aggressively, you will have more opportunity to gain what you want.

Great accomplishment seems incomplete,

yet its use is not impaired.

Great fullness seems empty,

yet it will never be drained.

Great straightness looks crooked.

Great skill appears clumsy.

Great eloquence sounds like stammering.

Movement overcomes cold,

stillness overcomes heat.

The calm and quiet set right

everything under heaven.

LAO-TZU

"We are not troubled by things, but by the opinion which we have of things."

EPICTETUS

Commitment

❝ What a man believes, he will die for. What a man merely thinks, he will change his mind about. ❞

ANONYMOUS

*Y*ou must do much more than read about wholeness and personal power. Intellectualizing is not doing. You must take positive action. Make a list of your goals, including your long-term ambitions, and turn them into affirmations. Re-reading your affirmations will help you to keep your goals present and activate your personal power. Affirmations also serve to help you overcome the negative expectations and habits you may have developed over the years with astoundingly positive effects. Try the following exercise for a month, and you will discover the power of affirmations.

Read your list aloud, prefacing each item with: *Without strain, hardship, or risk to my health, I positively intend*.... Do this at least once a day for a full month. You may find that you have your list memorized before the month ends. If so you may choose to revisit your list when you

❝If you are unsure of a course of action, do not attempt it. Your doubts and hesitations will infect your execution. Timidity is dangerous: Better to enter with boldness. Any mistakes you commit through audacity are easily corrected with more audacity. Everyone admires the bold; no one honors the timid.❞

ROBERT GREENE

A boy playing in the fields got stung by a nettle. He ran home to his mother, telling her that he had touched that nasty weed, and it had stung him. "It was just your touching it, my boy," said the mother, "that caused it to sting you; the next time you meddle with a nettle, grasp it tightly, and it will do you no hurt." Do boldly what you do at all.

AESOP

have a few moments alone. Every time you recite your intentions, you send a clear message into the universe. When you clearly state your goals, your actions will fall into line. You will become more mindful of how you must act to achieve them. With clarity of intent and purposeful action it can only be a matter of time before you see positive results. You may choose to continue using this tool, updating the list as time passes, and modifying it in the light of changed circumstances and successes.

Learn to be grateful and generous with your goods and your time.

Realize that you cannot gain from another's lack, and no one can hold you back but yourself. As you begin to work on your goals, include anyone who depends on you in your plans. Offer loved ones a chance to discuss any changes you would like to make. You have a team of ready allies there; do not alienate them. In remaining mindful of the feelings and needs of others, you remain connected to your own feeling nature. This awareness gives you access to your true personal power. If you fear that others may hold you back, recognize that you have created that "truth" and given it strength. In reality, your belief can hold you back but no one else can. Why blame others? Take responsibility for your own choices and life situation. You are here because you have a lesson to learn.

You cannot hit two targets with one arrow. If your thoughts stray, you miss the enemy's heart. Mind and arrow must become one. Only with such concentration of mental and physical power can your arrow hit the target and pierce the heart.

BALTASAR GRACIÁN

Work in Progress

Positive Speech

" *Man is what he believes.* "

ANTON CHEKHOV

Certain tasks become easier when you have a sense of your own personal power. Positive speech is important in both private interactions and public presentations. When meeting and speaking with others, make eye contact to convey your confidence and your interest in what the other person has to say. If this does not come easily to you, try the following.

When you make eye contact, vary where you look. Holding an intense gaze can seem intimidating. Instead, look the other person in the eyes, but alternate your focus from one eye to the other periodically. You might also glance at the mouth and other features before returning your contact to the eyes. This allows you to convey a sense of interest without hostility. Keep this odd fact in mind: It can be easier to look at someone's left eye than the right. For some reason, focusing on another's left eye is less confronting. Some say that this eye reflects the soul, while the right eye reveals the self we project to the world. Perhaps for this reason we feel more comfortable with another's left eye, and more easily rebuffed by the worldly-wise right.

❝ *The Master has no possessions. The more he does for others, the happier he is. The more he gives to others, the wealthier he is. The Tao nourishes by not forcing. By not dominating, the Master leads.* ❞

LAO-TZU

93

Many things which seemed important (at the time) turn out to be of no account when they are ignored; and others which seem trifling, appear formidable when you pay attention to them. Things can easily be settled at the outset, but not so later on. In many cases, the remedy itself is the cause of the disease: to let things be is not the least satisfactory of life's rules.

BALTASAR GRACIÁN

If you are naturally shy and find it difficult to make eye contact at all, another technique may help. Focus on the bridge of the nose, right between the eyes, or on the forehead just above the eyes. This will give the impression that you are making eye contact. With time, you may feel comfortable enough to shift your gaze to the eyes.

When speaking with others be aware of your own needs, strengths, and weaknesses. Be generous in your promises toward others, but don't make promises you don't intend to keep. Accept the risk that remaining true to yourself and honest in your dealings may involve disappointing others. Honesty and Awareness involve exercising your will, but they also validate others, which affirms your integrity.

66 *What one has, one ought to use; and whatever he does, he should do with all his might.* 99

CICERO

95

Walk Tall

66 Optimism is the faith that leads to achievement.
Nothing can be done without hope and confidence. 99

HELEN KELLER

*I*f you wish to experience and convey your personal power, walk tall. This has nothing to do with your physical stature but everything to do with how you feel about yourself. Imagine a thread that passes up your spine and out through the crown of your head. The end of the thread disappears into the sky, held by a mysterious, unseen hand. This imaginary thread will remind you to walk and sit tall, to keep your shoulders back and relaxed, your eyes forward and chin up, and your spine in a comfortable straight line. When you slouch, you inhibit your chest's capacity and limit your oxygen intake. This takes its toll, both mental and physical. If you have no medical conditions to preclude it (check with your physician if in doubt), exercise regularly to loosen your joints and to improve your posture. The Alexander Technique and Tai Chi are excellent methods for improving posture if you are able to find a skilled teacher.

66 *Confidence is that feeling by which the mind embarks on great and honorable courses with a sure hope and trust in itself.* 99

CICERO

66 *Never bend your head. Hold it high. Look the world straight in the eye.* **99**

HELEN KELLER

Speak with Confidence

"As soon as you trust yourself,
you will know how to live."

JOHANN WOLFGANG VON GOETHE

Consider next how you sound to others. Do you speak with authority or is your voice hesitant, shrill, or monotonous? Do you sound apologetic, rushed, nervous? Do you drone on atonally and bore your listeners? A less than confident voice lessens your personal power and may cause you to lose respect. If possible, record yourself reading aloud, ideally to an audience. Listen critically to the result. Do you like the way you sound?

Before your next speech, presentation, or important interview, try out the following experiment. You will need privacy and a timepiece with a minute and a second hand. If you have a stop-watch, so much the better.

- Choose a familiar topic and speak as though to your intended audience.
- Note the time when you begin to speak, but thereafter do not look at your watch.
- Talk for one minute.
- When you believe that a minute has elapsed, stop talking and immediately check the time. How accurate is your assessment of passing time?

Repeat this exercise.
- Again note the time you begin.
- This time remain silent until you estimate one minute has elapsed.
- Immediately check the time. How accurate were you this time?

Most people will find that they overestimate the passing of time, especially in the absence of noise. Anxiety and insecurity make us believe that we have taken too much of our listeners' time. Subsequently we hasten our speech. If silently awaiting feedback or taking time to craft a response, insecurity can make the wait seem far longer than it is.

Take this lesson to heart and slow down when you deliver a presentation or consider a response. In your nervousness, what seems like normal speech can sound like anxious babble to listeners. Take the time to think before you reply to a question. No one will wonder at a thirty-second pause, or more, before you answer, especially if you preface the pause with, "Let me think..." or something similar.

Remember to collect your thoughts and decide what you want to say before you open your mouth. Make what you say more powerful by speaking thoughtfully and in a controlled manner. Here are a few more tips for exercising your personal power in public:

- Remember that speaking in public or enduring an interview is an unnatural act; most people in these situations experience some nervousness. A good speaker remains in control despite that nervousness. The secret is to prepare. Know who you will be speaking to, why they invited you, and what they expect to learn from you. You may feel exposed, but you are not under attack. You possess information that your audience wants to hear.

- When working from documents, put them in order and fasten them together so they will not scatter if dropped.

- Know your subject so you do not have to rely too heavily on prepared material. A read speech can be both monotonous and embarrassing to witness. When you use electronic presentation tools, make sure to rehearse with them.

- Take a few deep breaths (subtly) before any difficult or important speech, then take your time with what you have to say. If you feel really anxious, discretely clench and unclench your fists, turn your head from side to side, and raise and lower your shoulders a few times to release tension before you approach your audience.

- Have your opening sentence rehearsed, and include an early humorous comment if appropriate. It will relax you and your audience.

- Thank your audience for coming, thank the organizers who invited you to speak, and thank the person who just introduced you. Find a "hook" to hold your listeners early. Do you have a witty or surprising fact or anecdote to share? I attended a conference recently where an excellent speaker pretended to be in a quandary over whether to tell an anecdote because it would involve shameless name-dropping. Overcoming his (mock) reticence, he revealed how he had recently tutored HM Queen Elizabeth, Queen of England, in the use of his product. It certainly got a laugh, and it garnered respectful attention.

Your icebreaking remarks should be genuine to be effective.

- Be prepared with a quip if you fluff a line. An excellent speaker turned a verbal slip to her advantage by merrily continuing, "I am so excited to be talking to you tonight the words are jostling to come out." Her warm and confident manner embraced the audience, endeared her to us, and saved us all from feeling embarrassed. You may need a different tactic according to your material and audience, but have a remark prepared.

- Avoid lists and statistics. Few people can absorb complex figures from a verbal presentation. Either present your audience with an electronic display or distribute the information on handouts.

- If your presentation might invite hostility from the audience, have a strategy prepared for dealing with hecklers. A tried and true method is to invite hecklers to share their thoughts from the stage. Many hecklers lose their bravado when removed from the security of an audience. (If someone takes you up on your offer, keep his or her remarks brief and politely resume control as soon as possible.) Alternatively, ask any hecklers to save their remarks for a question and answer session after your speech. Have offensive hecklers removed if you can, but beware of losing your audience's sympathy.

- Learn to moderate your tone. Most of us speak faster and in a higher register than normal when we feel anxious. Do as the politicians do: deliberately lower your voice and speak more slowly. A lower tone conveys more authority and commands greater respect than one in a higher register. A lower tone will also project further, with or without amplification. To avoid appearing comical, do not exaggerate your adjustment. Practice with a tape recorder or a tame audience, if possible.

- Pause occasionally for dramatic effect or for audience response to your humorous asides. When you can hold a moment's silence in this way, you reveal your control and power over the situation. If your audience senses your comfort, they will feel at ease too. It is discomforting to watch someone squirm.

- Ask for questions at the end of your speech and pay attention to them. Relief at finishing your speech may nearly overwhelm you, but until you have responded to questions, you still hold the stage. If someone asks you something that you cannot readily answer, have the courage to say so: "I do not have that information, but I will find out for you." If you promise to follow up on something, keep your promise.

- Keep your comments brief.

Examine Your Attitudes

❝ The passing moment is all we can be sure of; it is only common sense to extract its utmost value from it. ❞

W. Somerset Maugham

Through every feeling we experience, we reconnect with our essence. But not all feelings are pleasurable, and our attitude can affect how we interpret them. For example, some mothers describe childbirth as a truly agonizing experience, but others recall it as a time of enormous intensity rather than pain. If we focus on, rather than shrink from, lesser pain, we have the ability to transform it into the sensation of heat. When we allow and closely examine feelings, even pain, we may be able to describe how we "see" their shape, size, or even color. What we can describe, we can influence. We may learn to reduce our experience of pain if we allow ourselves to actually experience it. If we can describe a sensation in terms of a size or color, we can further practice imagining it as getting smaller or fading away.

Similarly, we can diminish our fears if we first allow ourselves to truly experience our feelings. We cannot change those things we label, externalize, or push away because in doing so we disassociate ourselves from them. How often have you become paralyzed at the thought of a situation yet found the actual experience much less painful or difficult than you anticipated? Look your fears "in the face" and learn their dimensions, color, location. You then know where to focus your will to cut it to size and control it. Respect your fears—some, such as a healthy respect for heights or deep water, actually protect you—but understand where they stem from and how much they hold you at their mercy.

**❝He
that would
have fruit
must climb
the tree.❞**

THOMAS FULLER

When we label a fact or experience, we distance ourselves from simply feeling it. What we label pain might seem more neutral if we focused on its source and observed it, rather than tensing and withdrawing from it. Neutrally observing any sensation opens us to experiencing life. The next time you start to shy away from strong feelings, allow yourself to fully experience them. Do so without judgment. Rather than using your thoughts to assess a situation, try using your feelings. (Begin by practicing this in stress-free, safe circumstances.) What we know, we can choose to change.

Always set to work without misgivings on the score of imprudence. Fear of failure in the mind of a performer is, for an onlooker, already evidence of failure. ... Actions are dangerous when there is doubt as to their wisdom; it would be safer to do nothing.

BALTASAR GRACIÁN

> There is no greater illusion than fear, no greater wrong than preparing to defend yourself, no greater misfortune than having an enemy.
>
> Whoever can see through all fear will always be safe.
>
> ANONYMOUS

All feelings, of whatever nature, connect our inner selves to the world. They are our experience of energy and power. Our personal power is no different. Unless we open ourselves up to feel our power, we cannot truly experience it. We even label and reject love as too dangerous if we deem the feelings it evokes too immense to bear. Many cling, childlike, to the known, even when the known has proven unsatisfactory. Our fear can prevent us from experiencing the love and potential for personal power present in all situations. When we prejudge and reject these sensations, we place ourselves apart from other people, never taking risks—never enjoying growth. We stay in the safe place, relationship, or job rather than risking the joy of something better.

Willpower

❝ Life is a bridge, cross over it but build no house on it. ❞

INDIAN PROVERB

Whenever we speak of "trying" to do this or that, we are also subtly acknowledging an expectation that we may fail. Learn to say that you *will do* rather than you *will try to do*. This is an important difference. Our outward expression reflects our inner commitment and intent. Learn to couch what you say in truly positive terms, and commit to following through. Not only will you reassure those with whom you interact, you will also subtly affect your own actions. For example, "I'd love to attend" reflects a genuine intent, rather than the weaker, "I hope to be there," or "I will try to make it." If something then genuinely prevents you from attending, you can explain the situation with truthful regret. If, on the other hand, you know you cannot commit to a course of action, do not say you will try. This is misleading and a dishonest way to curry favor, one that will point out to others that you lack the personal power to refuse because you fear the consequences. Hollow promises soon wear thin. Exercise your right to decline, or clearly state what you must do before you can make a commitment. You will be regarded more favorably for being aware and in control of your true availability. Don't give in to the temptation to say what you hope will make you popular, or what you think others want to hear, when you know you cannot keep your word. This is more than good policy. Saying what you mean is the first step to getting what you want.

Evaluation

66 *Only those means of security are good, are certain, are lasting, that depend on yourself and your own vigor.* **99**

NICCOLÒ MACHIAVELLI

*T*ime to take stock.

- *Awareness*—Reflect on your feelings concerning personal power. Discover your strengths and weaknesses. Use relaxation and creative imagination techniques if necessary. Consider how you would live in an ideal world. Why do you refuse personal power now? Pay attention to your intuition and dreams.

- *Assessment*—Truthfully look at your current situation. What have you got to deal with right now? What opportunities and resources are available to you? Who can you call on for help? How might you incorporate your talents and ideals into your life? How can you find out more about your interests?

- *Action*—Balance the creative and practical aspects of your nature for more effective action. Acknowledge your right to personal power. Review the insights and experience you have gained and assess their practical worth. Set goals and work to achieve them. Monitor your progress and update your goals. If you doubt your right or ability to exercise personal power, you may need some simple successes to help you believe that you have what it takes. Begin to extend yourself and gain those successes. Appropriate action for you may be the act of letting go, not of striving.

You cannot learn new skills merely by attending lectures. Skills require practice. You will not become a different person overnight just because you read this book or another like it. Take the next step—that's enough. You do not have to become the next Einstein or Marie Curie. The real you will do just fine.

According to Chinese tradition, Lao-Tzu disciples were traveling through a forest one day where hundreds of trees had been cleared. In the center stood a huge tree with hundreds of branches. Woodcutters rested in its shade. The disciples asked the woodcutters why they had left the tree standing.

"Because it is absolutely useless. The bark is so tough, it breaks our saws. And even if we are able to chop off a piece, the smoke it makes when burned stings our eyes."

When the disciples reported this conversation to Lao-Tzu, he laughed.

"Be like this tree. Be absolutely useless. If you become useful, somebody will come along and make a chair out of you. Be like this tree and you will be left alone to grow big and full, and thousands of people will come to rest under your shade."

Any process of change involves:

1. Self-awareness, to identify beneficial changes and the desire for change.

2. Commitment to act differently in the future.

3. The opportunity to enact your new resolve.

4. The courage to follow through.

5. The will to evaluate the results. What worked well and what not so well? How might you do better next time? What did you learn? How did your new behavior affect others?

With personal power comes a real spirit of generosity. True generosity reflects the giver's desire to increase the pleasure of another and the belief that the selected gift will do so. True giving occurs without reluctance or any wish to control the fate of the gift. The act of giving is complete and pure; it harbors no expectation of reciprocal action. When we give gifts freely and honestly, we open ourselves to opportunity to receive from the universe.

Coping with Disappointment

66 When two great forces oppose each other, the victory will go to the one that knows how to yield. 99

LAO-TZU

Things go wrong; that is just a fact of life. Learning always involves trial and error, which is actually an efficient learning tool. You try a bit and succeed, and you feel good about yourself. Then you try again and fail. This is your big chance—your chance to evaluate and learn. What went wrong? What needs to change to succeed next time? If you never encountered problems, how could you gauge your progress? Everyone learns this way. Your greatest hero or heroine grew through failure and disappointment. Failure is the strength behind all personal experience. What disables us is the fear of failure. Once you have failed and survived (as you will 99.9 percent of the time), you become stronger for the knowledge you have gained. Because fear magnifies problems, you will discover that you have less to lose than you anticipated. Let go and get on with living. Stop trying to control things. Those efforts to remain in control actually create anxiety. No matter what, you will fail sometimes. Accept it. You will be better for it.

How do you cope with disappointments and failures? Do you see them as markers on the road or as gates slammed in your face? Do you blame others? Perhaps you deny failure and pass the blame to avoid having your weakness revealed.

> As some make gossip out of everything, so others make much ado about everything. They are always talking big, [and] take everything seriously, making a quarrel and a mystery of it. You should take very few grievances to heart, for to do so is to give yourself groundless worry. It is a topsy—turvy way of behaving to take to heart cares which you ought to throw over your shoulder.
>
> BALTASAR GRACIÁN

Success and

How to Cope with It

66 *The greatest danger occurs at the moment of victory.* **99**

NAPOLEON BONAPARTE

Can you accept success, or do you still nurse a belief that you cannot have or do not deserve it? There is no surer way to cut yourself off from the experience.

A man who was famous as a tree-climber was guiding someone in climbing a tall tree. He ordered the man to cut the top branches, and, during this time, when the man seemed to be in great danger, the expert said nothing. Only when the man was coming down and had reached the height of the eaves did the expert call out, "Be careful! Watch your step coming down!" I asked him, "Why did you say that? At that height he could jump the rest of the way if he chose."

"That's the point," said the expert. "As long as the man was up at a dizzy height and the branches were threatening to break, he himself was so afraid I said nothing. Mistakes are always made when people get to the easy places."

KENKÔ

Do you believe even now that any success that you have had is a fluke? Are you afraid that someone will expose you as a fraud? If you do not understand how you "lucked" into success the first time, it is unlikely to happen again. But stop and think for a moment. Did you have luck or did you set objectives and work hard to achieve them? Perhaps you feel as though your success was too easily attained to trust that you might repeat it. Have you always believed that people have to suffer in order to get good things? Perhaps you believe that achievement only follows trials and suffering? What do you think now? More to the point, what do you feel?

❝ *My success is measured by my willingness to keep trying.* ❞

ANONYMOUS

Accept Praise

❝ Here is a test to find whether your mission on earth is finished: If you're alive, it isn't. ❞

RICHARD BACH

When someone freely offers praise or pays you a compliment, you honor the bestower with your gracious acceptance but cause embarrassment when you reject it. Instead, why not thank the giver without protestations or false modesty? Do you feel that others will have a lower opinion of you if you do not deflect praise? You may be surprised; you will be liked just as well. In fact, you may be liked even more, as the praise-giver can now feel good about his or her generosity. No one has forced this genuine expression of praise. In warmly thanking the praise-giver for a kind remark you are in effect applauding another's good judgment and sensibilities. Acquire the habit of giving praise to those who sincerely earn it. It will help you to accept it gracefully when it comes your way.

> ❝ *It is not necessarily those lands which are the most fertile or most favored in climate that seem to me the happiest, but those in which a long struggle of adaptation between man and his environment has brought out the best qualities of both.* ❞
>
> **T. S. ELIOT**

Picture Credits

cover: Jacob Sutton (Contemporary artist) Private Collection/Bridgeman Art Library.

pages 2 and 109: English School (16th century) Private Collection/Bridgeman Art Library.

page 10: Keisai Eizan (1787–1867) Victoria & Albert Museum, London/Bridgeman Art Library.

page 22: Giuseppe Pellizza da Volpedo (1868–1907) Private Collection/Bridgeman Art Library.

page 30: English School (19th century) Bonhams, London/Bridgeman Art Library.

page 38: Sven Richard Bergh (1858–1919) Goteborgs Konstmuseum, Sweden/Bridgeman Art Library.

page 47: Paul Gauguin (1848–1903) Musée d'Orsay, Paris/Bridgeman Art Library.

page 54: Chinese School (19th century) Phillips, The International Fine Art Auctioneers, UK/Bridgeman Art Library.

page 62: Paul Cézanne (1839–1906) Buhrle Collection Zurich/Bridgeman Art Library.

page 70: Patricia O'Brien (Contemporary artist) Private Collection/Bridgeman Art Library.

page 78: Caspar David Friedrich (1774–1840) Schloss Sanssouci, Potsdam/Bildarchiv Steffens/Bridgeman Art Library.

page 84: William Powell Frith (1819–1909) Royal Albert Memorial Museum, Exeter, Devon/Bridgeman Art Library.

page 90: From 15th-century manuscript, Histoire Universelle (c. 1286) British Library/Bridgeman Art Library.

page 99: Wilhelm List (1864–1918) Whitford & Hughes, London/Bridgeman Art Library.

page 114: Pierre Auguste Renoir (1841–1919) The Barnes Foundation, Merion, Pennsylvania/ Bridgeman Art Library.

page 125: Henry Scheffer (1798–1862) Chateau de Versailles/Bridgeman Art Library.

Text Credits & References

page 63: Julia Cameron *Recovering Your Creative Self*, Pan 1995.

page 53: Dorothy Law Nolte *Children Learn What They Live. Parenting to Inspire Values*, Workman Publishing Company 1988.

pages 27, 37, 87: Robert Greene *The 48 Laws of Power*, Profile Books 1998.

page 118: Carol Orsborn ©1992 *Inner Excellence: Spiritual Principles of Life-Driven Business*. Used with permission from New World Library, Novato, CA 94949, *www.newworldlibrary.com*

pages 24, 28, 29, 41, 95, 111, 120: Stephen Mitchell *Tao Te Ching: A New English Version*, HarperCollins 1989.